PEOPLE AT WORK

AT A VET'S

DEBORAH FOX

Evans

EVANS BROTHERS LIMITED

Published by Evans Brothers Limited
2a Portman Mansions
Chiltern Street
London
W1M 1LE

First published in 1998

Commissioned by: Su Swallow
Design: Neil Sayer
Photographer: Gareth Boden
Illustrator: Liam Bonney/The Art Market

British Library Cataloguing in Publication Data

Fox, Deborah
  People at work in a vet's
  1.Veterinarians - Juvenile 2.Veterinary medicine - Juvenile
  literature
  I.Title
  636'.089

ISBN 0237518244

Printed in Hong Kong by Wing King Tong

Acknowledgements

The author and publisher wish to thank the following for their
help:
Susie Russell, Joyce Murray and the team at Runnymede Hill
Animal Hospital, Egham, Surrey; Stephen and Zyllah Cooke,
Colin Blakey and the team at Kelperlands Veterinary Centre,
Touchen End, Berkshire; Carl Boyde of Boyde and Partners,
Staines, Middlesex; Reptech; Tim Heron and the staff at Swan
Lifeline, Cuckoo Weir Island, Eton, Berkshire.

All photographs by Gareth Boden except for pages 26 and 27
by Chris Heatley.

Contents

The veterinary team

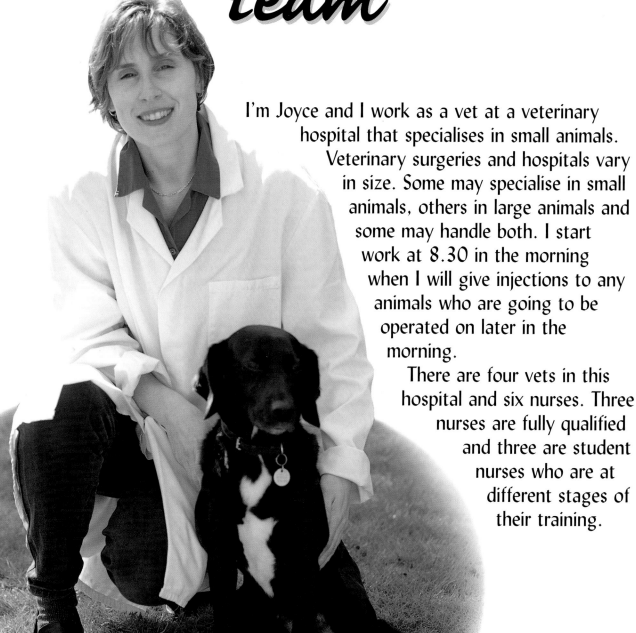

I'm Joyce and I work as a vet at a veterinary hospital that specialises in small animals. Veterinary surgeries and hospitals vary in size. Some may specialise in small animals, others in large animals and some may handle both. I start work at 8.30 in the morning when I will give injections to any animals who are going to be operated on later in the morning.

There are four vets in this hospital and six nurses. Three nurses are fully qualified and three are student nurses who are at different stages of their training.

Part of the nursing team. Not all nurses are on duty at the same time, as we need to make sure we are covered during our opening hours from 9am until 7pm.

The vet checks an animal's history on his computer.

Consultations

People make appointments for the vets to see their animals as we are always so busy, but if there is an emergency then we will always see the animal. Our consultations are from 9am until 12.30pm and then again from 4.15pm until 7pm. Other surgeries may have slightly different hours to ours. We keep records of all the animals we see on computer so that they can easily be called up when the animals come in again.

I did a degree at university in veterinary science for five years. After that I joined a small practice with just one other vet.

In the consulting room

There are special consulting rooms where we see the animals and their owners. The owners explain to us what is wrong with their pets and we try to find out, or diagnose, what the problems are. Some illnesses are straightforward and can be treated quite easily, but other problems might be harder to diagnose.

▼ *Animals cannot speak for themselves and so it is important for me to gather every bit of information on the pet's symptoms.*

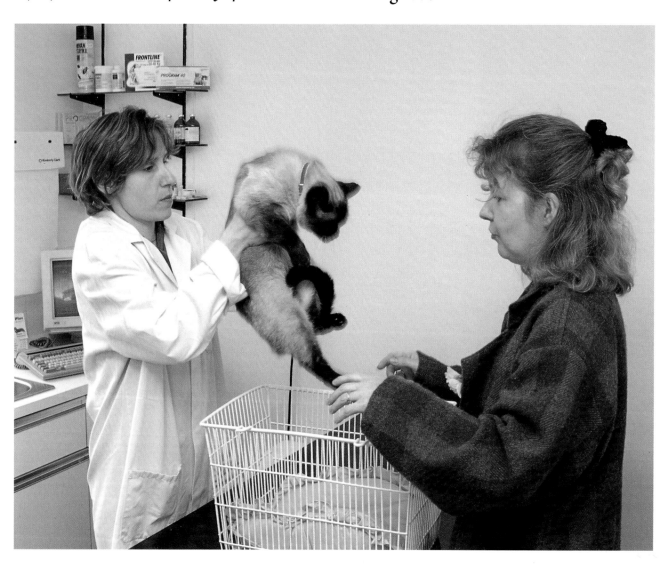

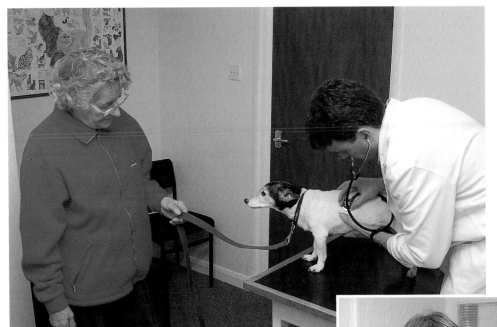

◀ The vet, Kevin, listens to Lorna's heart to check if the heartbeat is normal.

▼ Gypsy's leg covering will be removed in a week's time when the leg should have healed.

A heart problem

Kevin sees a Jack Russell dog called Lorna, who is thirteen years old. Lorna comes to us quite frequently because she has a heart problem. She is having breathing problems and also some fits. The vet listens to Lorna's heart with his stethoscope. The heartbeat is quite noisy and not normal and so the vet decides to adjust Lorna's dosage of tablets. He asks her owner to come in again so that he can check on her condition in a week's time.

Car accidents

Vets often see cats and dogs who have been injured in car accidents. Gypsy was hit by a car and has a broken leg.

To repair the leg, the vet, Stephen, had to insert three stainless steel pins into and around the joint and a stainless steel wire to hold the pins together. The protective cover is there to try to stop Gypsy using her leg too much so that it will heal properly. The treatment takes about three weeks altogether and after that time, the vet will decide if he can remove the pins.

Diagnosing the problems

Some vets will see some quite unusual animals. Two swans from a sanctuary have been brought in to see Stephen, who specialises in treating birds. One swan, Hawker, has a deformed wing and the other, Lennon, is extremely ill.

Diagnosis

Vets diagnose what is wrong with sick animals, based on what the owners tell them, the symptoms the animals have,

▼ Hawker and Lennon in the waiting room.

their years of study and their experience of treating animals. Hawker will need to have part of his wing amputated and so he is admitted to have an operation. The vet is concerned about Lennon's symptoms, which suggest that he is suffering from lead poisoning.

Confirming diagnosis

Stephen takes a blood sample from Lennon and tests it on a special machine that can detect the level of lead in the blood. After three minutes the results come through. As the vet suspects, the lead in Lennon's blood is extremely high. If the vet had to send away the blood sample to be tested in a laboratory, then he would lose vital days that could be spent on treatment.

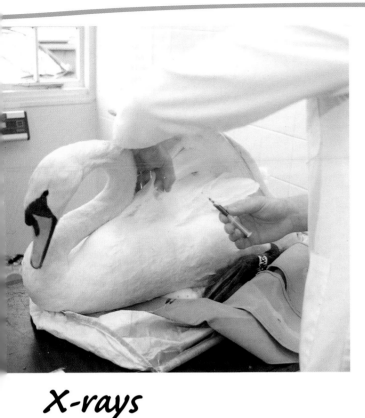

◁ The vet takes a blood sample to test for lead poisoning.

▽ The vet prepares Lennon for the X-ray. All X-rays are done in a separate room for safety.

X-rays

The vet takes an X-ray to check if he can see the lead because the people at the sanctuary believe Lennon has swallowed lead near the river. X-rays are vital for checking the internal organs of animals.

Lead poisoning in swans

- Low, droopy neck held right back on the body instead of being upright
- Weak or thin pulse
- Muscle wastage
- Dehydration
- Eyes not wide and circular but olive-shaped
- Green staining near the tail
- Foul smell from beak

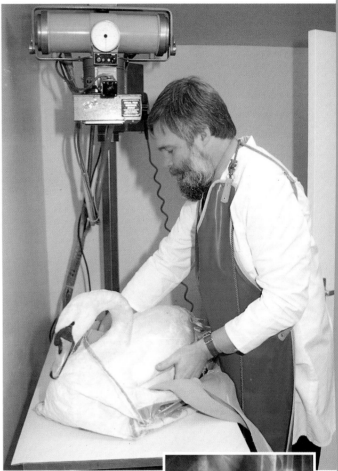

▷ Lennon seems to have swallowed lead pellets from an old gun cartridge. The vet will need to flush the lead through Lennon's system by inserting a tube down his throat to wash out the lead.

In the 'prep' room

We carry out routine work on the animals – work that doesn't involve a serious operation – in the 'prep' room, or preparation room. This is where the nurses prepare the injections, where we give sedatives, where we do any dental work on animals and any post-operative procedures. We refer to this as 'post-op' work, meaning anything that has to be done after an operation.

◀ *This nurse prepares the sedatives or 'pre-meds' (pre-medications), which calm down the animal. The vets give the animals their pre-meds about an hour before the operation.*

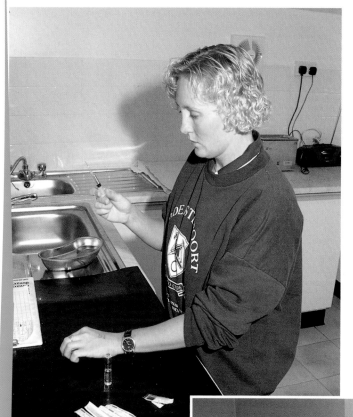

▶ *Sarah, the head nurse, is trained to perform simple surgery on animals that does not involve going inside an animal's body. Here she removes a cyst, or growth, from a dog's neck, watched by a student nurse.*

Nurses

Nurses keep the surgery running smoothly. They keep detailed records of which animals we will be operating on, their names and their owners' names, their weights, and which sedatives or painkillers we have given. Each animal has its own cage or kennel with its own chart on the door.

> I enjoy being a veterinary nurse because every day is different. I get so much satisfaction from seeing a sick or injured animal being nursed back to health.
>
> Michelle, veterinary nurse

Training to be a nurse

The training can take two or three years. Nurses can train at a veterinary practice or hospital and go to college for one day every week. They can train more quickly if they spend three months at a college during the first year, followed by another three months in the second year.

▼ Michelle fills in details on the treatment given to a cat on its chart. Keeping records up to date is vital. Anyone checking on the cat later in the day can find out what treatment he has had and at what time.

Preparing for operations

I need to perform a routine operation on a dog called Zoe, who is three years old. She has already had her pre-med early this morning. After I have given her the anaesthetic, the nurse hooks her up to the anaesthetic machine. She makes sure that Zoe has the correct level of anaesthetic to keep her asleep throughout the operation.

▲ I inject Zoe with an anaesthetic. During the operation the nurse checks the level of anaesthetic on a machine.

▶ CJ, the nurse, shaves the area I will be operating on. She then uses an antiseptic liquid to make sure the area is clean.

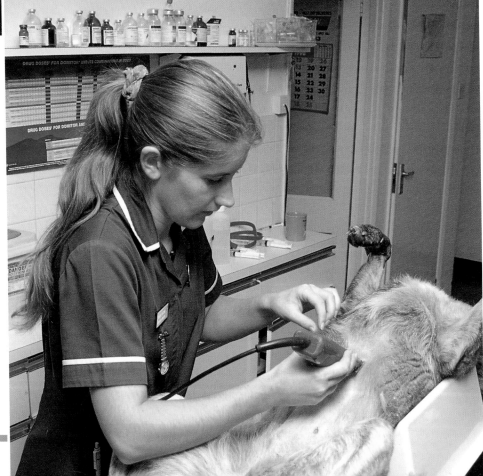

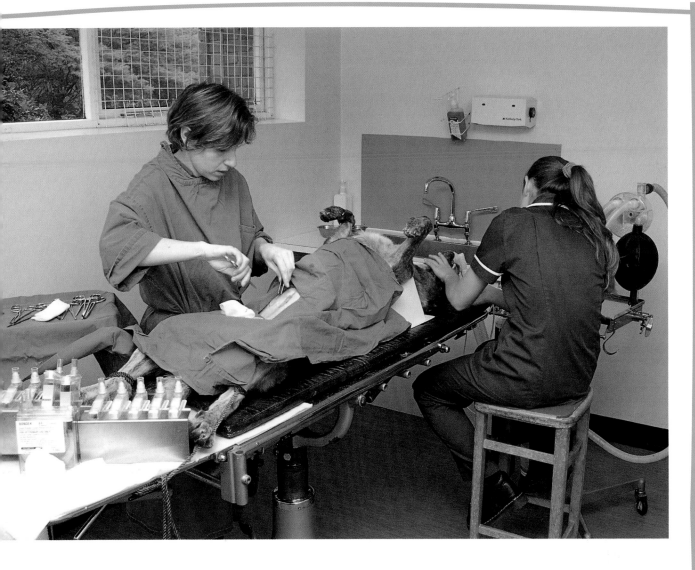

Taking her to theatre

Because Zoe is quite heavy we have a special 'trough' or 'cradle' we put her in so that she can't roll over. Then the nurses lift her on to a trolley and wheel her through to theatre. This is a sterile room where everything is kept extremely clean to avoid any risk of infection to the animals. Nurses assist in the operations, making sure the animals are comfortable and breathing normally.

▲ The nurse checks that Zoe is getting a good supply of oxygen and that she is breathing normally.

I put drapes, green covers, round the area I am going to operate on. I make a small incision, or cut, into Zoe which means I can remove her ovaries. This means she won't be able to have puppies. This operation is known as a 'dog spay'. It is a straightforward operation and doesn't take too long. I then sew up the cut.

In theatre

Before operations vets always 'scrub up' to get rid of any germs on their hands and arms. Using a special anti-bacterial soap, the vet brushes each finger in turn – usually five scrubs per finger – until both hands have been thoroughly cleaned, as well as the arms. All vets wear a clean, green surgical gown for every operation.

Operating on the swan

After the anaesthetic, Hawker is carried to the operating table to have his 'airplane wing' (see page 19) removed. The vet, Stephen, cuts away

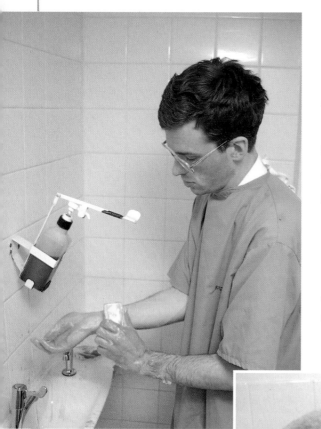

▲ It is important not to let the arms drop when they are wet as any bacteria will run down on to the hands.

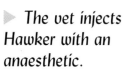

▶ The vet injects Hawker with an anaesthetic.

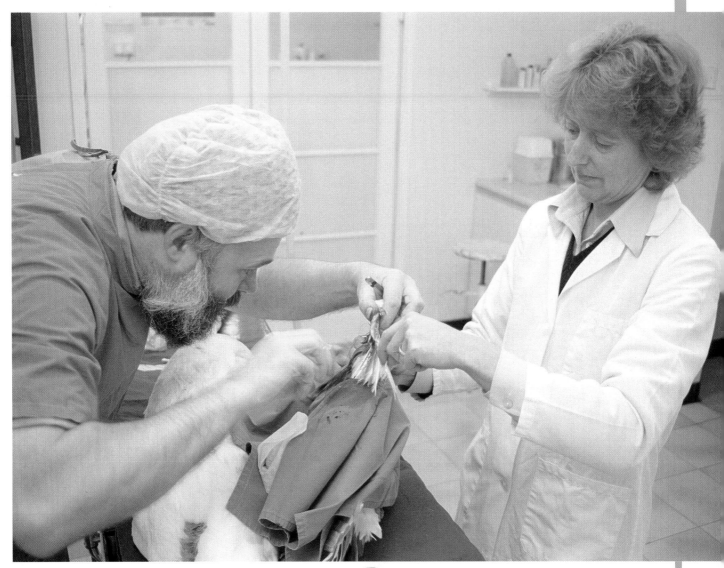

▲ The vet removes the deformed wing tip. Hawker's brother, Concorde, also suffered from the condition known as airplane wing. Both his wings were damaged.

the damaged feathers at the tip of the wing. After half an hour, Stephen sews up the repaired wing and bandages it to keep it clean as it heals. Hawker is taken to a kennel where he can recover from the operation.

Airplane wing

When the outer ten feathers of a swan's wing have twisted round, this condition is known as 'airplane' or 'angel wing'. The damaged part of the wing has to be removed. Even though the swan won't be able to fly, he will be able to live a normal life.

Dental work

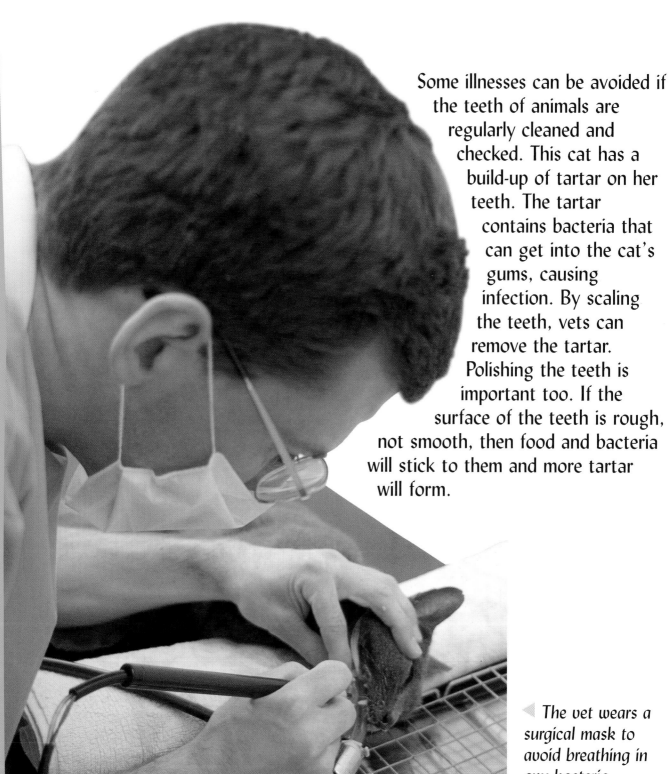

Some illnesses can be avoided if the teeth of animals are regularly cleaned and checked. This cat has a build-up of tartar on her teeth. The tartar contains bacteria that can get into the cat's gums, causing infection. By scaling the teeth, vets can remove the tartar. Polishing the teeth is important too. If the surface of the teeth is rough, not smooth, then food and bacteria will stick to them and more tartar will form.

◀ The vet wears a surgical mask to avoid breathing in any bacteria.

After the operations

The nurses thoroughly clean and disinfect the operating theatre after each operation. They wash the operating gowns, clean the instruments and then pack them into individual bags. Each bag contains all the instruments we need for routine surgical procedures. Before putting these kits into the sterilising machine, the nurses make sure that they are airtight to stop them bursting open.

▲ There are different-sized kits. The standard-sized ones are for routine procedures and the larger ones are for more difficult operations.

▲ Keeping all parts of the surgery clean and tidy is essential. Michelle cleans the theatre after Hawker's operation.

It's really important for owners to clean the teeth of their pets on a daily basis. Imagine what your teeth would be like if you hadn't cleaned them for five or six years!

Colin, vet

Going home

A few hours after the operation, Hawker is well enough to go back to the sanctuary. His wings need to be secured so that he does not attempt to flap them on his way home. After three days his bandage will be removed and he will fully recover within ten days.

▶ Hawker is wrapped in a special 'swan wrap' to keep his wings and legs in place.

▽ The volunteers at the swan sanctuary will place Hawker with other disabled swans so that he can find a mate.

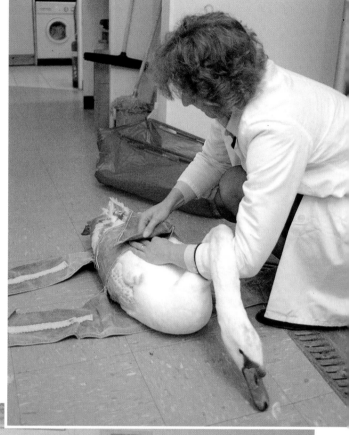

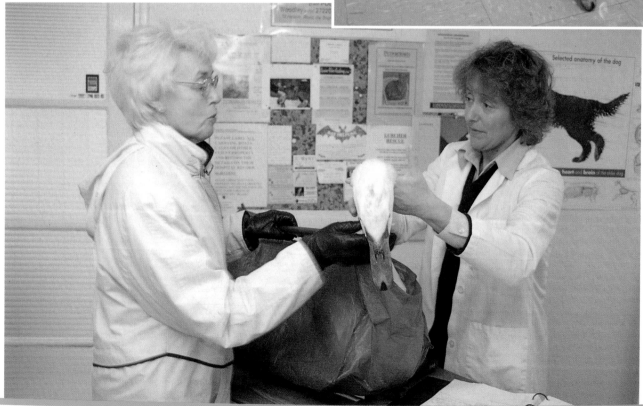

Recovering

Zoe is recovering from her operation. As she comes round from the anaesthetic, she starts to twitch a little. It takes about two hours before she will feel steady enough to go home. The nurses check on the condition of Zoe as she recovers in the kennels.

Administration

Veterinary nurses are responsible for keeping detailed notes on all the animals and the costs of their treatment. They also check that we are well stocked with all the medicines and equipment we need.

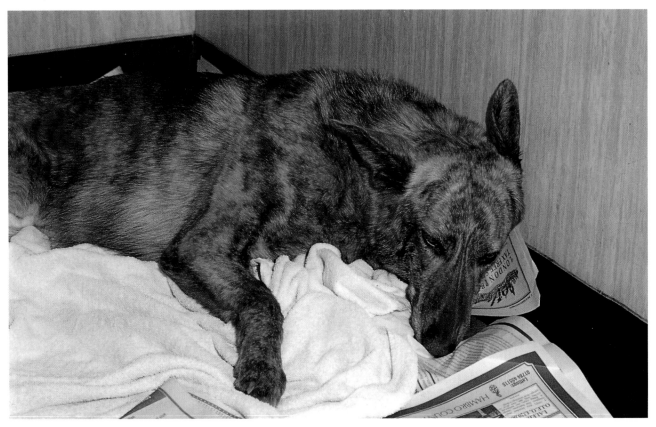

▲ Zoe starts to twitch as she comes round from the anaesthetic. Other dogs shake or start to 'paddle' with their legs.

Large animals

Some vets see both large and small animals and some specialise in large animals. Often it is more sensible for the vet to visit the animal at its home as it is so much harder to transport a large animal to a vet's. Vets see a wide variety of farm animals, such as cows, pigs, horses and sheep. They all need regular check-ups.

Lambs

A lamb's mother, the ewe, is vaccinated against many diseases that can affect both herself and her lamb, such as tetanus.

▼ *The vet examines the goat to see whether he is suffering from mange mites or lice.*

Unusual animals

Vets may get asked to check on more unusual animals too. This Ugandan cow grows fairly long horns. The vet checks that the horns are warm, which indicates that she is not suffering from the cold. In the winter months she is covered by a blanket to keep her warm.

▲ The vet makes sure that this newborn lamb is feeding well.

▶ This Ugandan cow is naturally lean with a russet-coloured coat. The vet checks her coat for lice and then he inspects the condition of her tail. Finally, he examines her feet to see if they need clipping.

Exotic animals

▼ Iggy is quite strong and has sharp claws, so the vet, Colin, has to handle him carefully. Iggy is about twelve years old and could live until he is about twenty.

Some vets specialise in exotic animals, such as lizards, fish, iguanas, snakes and spiders.

Iggy, the iguana

The biggest problem vets find with iguanas is weak bones because their owners aren't giving their pet the right diet and adequate light. Iguanas need ultra-violet light. Without it their bones weaken because they lack calcium.

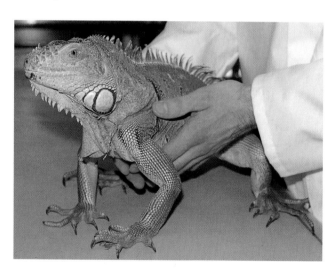

▶ Colin examines Iggy's head and the condition of his skin.

No-one should ever hold an iguana by its tail because it can drop off. It will re-grow, but it will never be as beautiful as the original tail.

Colin, specialist in exotic animals

▲ Jack is about three metres long. The vet is careful not to hold on to him any longer than necessary as snakes don't like to be restrained.

Jack, the boa constrictor

Colin checks the head and then the mouth of this boa constrictor because snakes can suffer from mouth rot, which is an infection of the mouth. Jack eats two rats once a week. If a rat's tooth cuts the snake's mouth it can cause infection. Jack, however, is fit and well with a lovely healthy skin. He sheds his skin every two months.

Glossary

anaesthetic a substance that causes numbness; it is used to prevent the feeling of pain during an operation

antiseptic a substance that prevents infection

bacteria very tiny living things that can cause infectious diseases in plants and animals

consultation a meeting between the vet and the patient to discuss the animal's symptoms of illness

dehydration the process of losing water from the body

internal organs the parts inside the body

lice (plural of louse) small wingless insects that live on some animals

mange a bad skin disease caused by mites; animals with mange itch and their hair can fall out

mites very tiny creatures that live on some animals

pre-medication a drug given to an animal before an operation to calm it down

sanctuary a place where animals can live and breed

sedative a drug used to calm or soothe an animal (see pre-medication)

symptoms signs of disease or illness

tartar a hard yellowish substance that forms on the teeth; it is caused by not cleaning teeth properly

tetanus a serious infectious disease

theatre the clean, sterile room where operations are carried out

ultra-violet light a type of light from the sun that is not visible; it can be produced by a special lamp

vaccinate to give an injection to protect against catching a disease

x-ray photograph of parts inside the body; bones show up well on x-rays

Index

Hawker and his brother, Concorde, remained at the santuary until a home with a lake could be found for them. Lennon recovered from the lead poisoning. Gypsy's leg healed. Lorna, unfortunately, died from old age and her heart condition. Zoe had her stiches removed and recovered well.